# Trailblazers in SPACE

by Charis Mather

Minneapolis, Minnesota

**Credits**
Images are courtesy of Shutterstock.com. With thanks to GettyImages, ThinkstockPhoto, and iStockphoto. Throughout – GoodStudio, mhatzapa. Cover – Azamatovic, denayunebgt, HilaryDesign, Tashal. 4–5, ProStockStudio, IYIKON; 6–7, Arto Jousi (WikiCommons), Vectorina; 8–9, Alexander Mokletsov (WikiCommons); 10–11, NASA (WikiCommons); 12–15, NASA (WikiCommons), sweet kiwi, charnsitr, Irina Strelnikova, badrus soleh, PremiumArt; 16–17, chinch, LynxVector, NASA (WikiCommons); 18–19, unknown (WikiComons); 20–21, NASA (WikiCommons); 22–23, BNP Design Studio.

**Bearport Publishing Company Product Development Team**
President: Jen Jenson; Director of Product Development: Spencer Brinker; Managing Editor: Allison Juda; Associate Editor: Naomi Reich; Senior Designer: Colin O'Dea; Associate Designer: Elena Klinkner; Associate Designer: Kayla Eggert; Product Development Specialist: Anita Stasson

*Library of Congress Cataloging-in-Publication Data*

Names: Mather, Charis, 1999- author.
Title: Trailblazers in space / by Charis Mather.
Description: Minneapolis, Minnesota : Bearport Publishing Company, [2024] | Series: Our greatest adventures | Includes index.
Identifiers: LCCN 2023002682 (print) | LCCN 2023002683 (ebook) | ISBN 9798885099585 (hardcover) | ISBN 9798888221334 (paperback) | ISBN 9798888222782 (ebook)
Subjects: LCSH: Astronauts--Biography--Juvenile literature.
Classification: LCC TL789.85.A1 M23 2024 (print) | LCC TL789.85.A1 (ebook) | DDC 629.450092--dc23/eng/20230124
LC record available at https://lccn.loc.gov/2023002682
LC ebook record available at https://lccn.loc.gov/2023002683

© 2024 BookLife Publishing
This edition is published by arrangement with BookLife Publishing.

North American adaptations © 2024 Bearport Publishing Company. All rights reserved. No part of this publication may be reproduced in whole or in part, stored in any retrieval system, or transmitted in any form or by any means, electronic, mechanical, photocopying, recording, or otherwise, without written permission from the publisher.

For more information, write to Bearport Publishing, 5357 Penn Avenue South, Minneapolis, MN 55419.

# CONTENTS

Our Greatest Adventures in Space .. 4
Yuri Gagarin.................... 6
Valentina Tereshkova .............. 8
Alexei Leonov................... 10
Neil Armstrong.................. 12
Buzz Aldrin..................... 14
Kathryn Sullivan ................. 16
Valery Vladimirovich Polyakov .... 18
You............................ 20
Your Space Adventure............ 22
Glossary....................... 24
Index .......................... 24

# OUR GREATEST ADVENTURES IN SPACE

For thousands of years, people looked up at the stars and wondered what they were seeing. But today, we are able to send people to space!

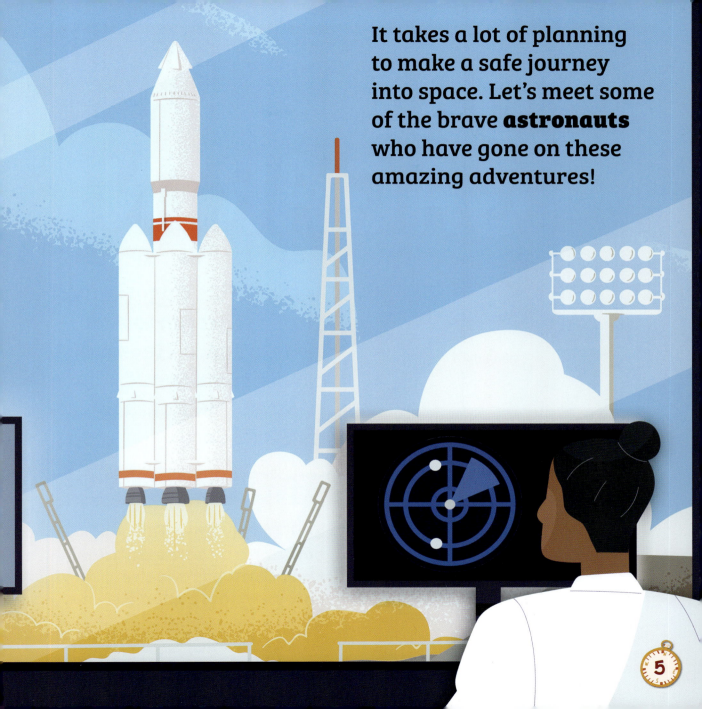

It takes a lot of planning to make a safe journey into space. Let's meet some of the brave **astronauts** who have gone on these amazing adventures!

# YURI GAGARIN

**Born: 1934**
**Died: 1968**

In 1961, Yuri Gagarin was the first person to ever go into space. He was a Soviet **cosmonaut** who **piloted** the first flight that left Earth.

Soviet is a word for someone or something that comes from the country now called Russia.

Yuri traveled around Earth once. His **spacecraft** then headed back down to Earth. A **parachute** slowed the craft down to a safe speed for landing.

## Be Inspired!

Never be afraid to be the first person to try something new.

# VALENTINA TERESHKOVA

**Born: 1937**

The first woman to go to space was cosmonaut Valentina Tereshkova. She was 26 years old at the time of her flight. To prepare for space, Valentina spent a lot of time using parachutes on Earth.

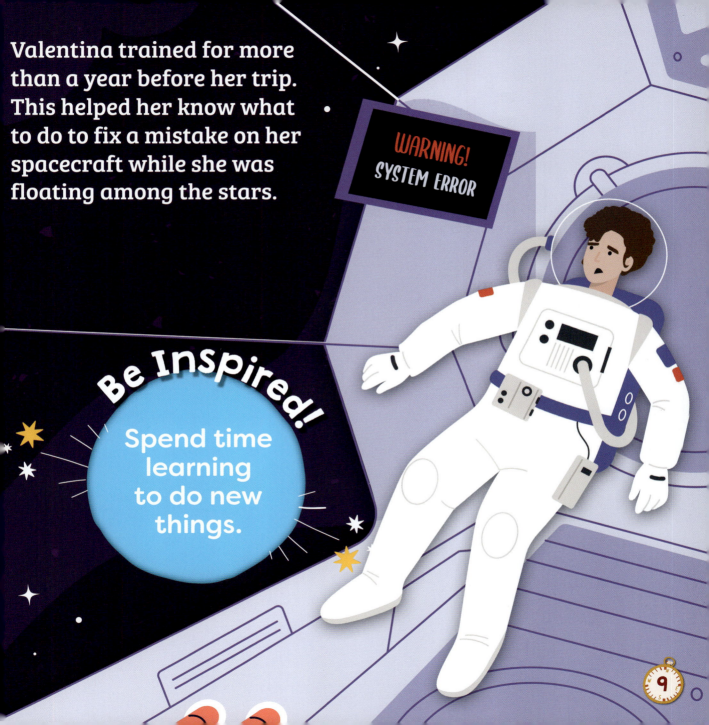

Valentina trained for more than a year before her trip. This helped her know what to do to fix a mistake on her spacecraft while she was floating among the stars.

WARNING! SYSTEM ERROR

**Be Inspired!** Spend time learning to do new things.

# ALEXEI LEONOV

**Born: 1934**
**Died: 2019**

Alexei Leonov was the first person to go on a **spacewalk**. He wore a special suit that let him leave his spacecraft for a short time.

Alexei was also the first person to make art in space.

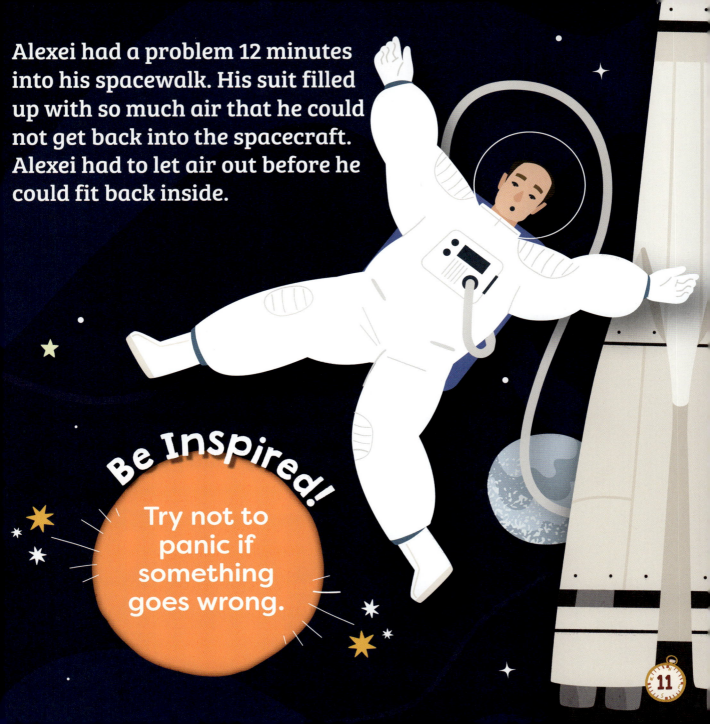

Alexei had a problem 12 minutes into his spacewalk. His suit filled up with so much air that he could not get back into the spacecraft. Alexei had to let air out before he could fit back inside.

## Be Inspired!

Try not to panic if something goes wrong.

# NEIL ARMSTRONG

**Born: 1930**
**Died: 2012**

The first man to walk on the moon was American astronaut Neil Armstrong. He was part of a **mission** to safely land people there.

Neil's mission was called *Apollo 11*.

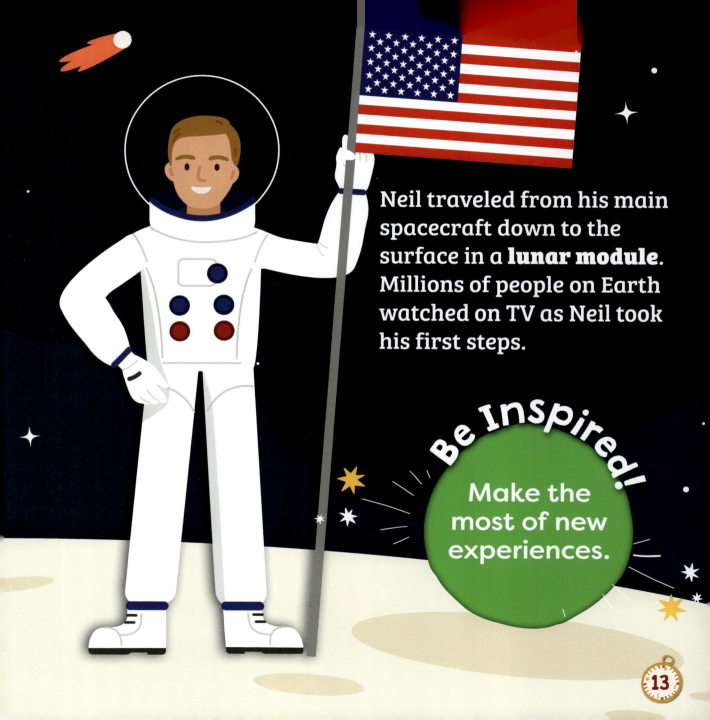

Neil traveled from his main spacecraft down to the surface in a **lunar module**. Millions of people on Earth watched on TV as Neil took his first steps.

## Be Inspired!
Make the most of new experiences.

# BUZZ ALDRIN

**Born: 1930**

Buzz Aldrin piloted the lunar module that took Neil to the moon. Buzz became the second person on the moon. He stepped on it about 20 minutes after Neil.

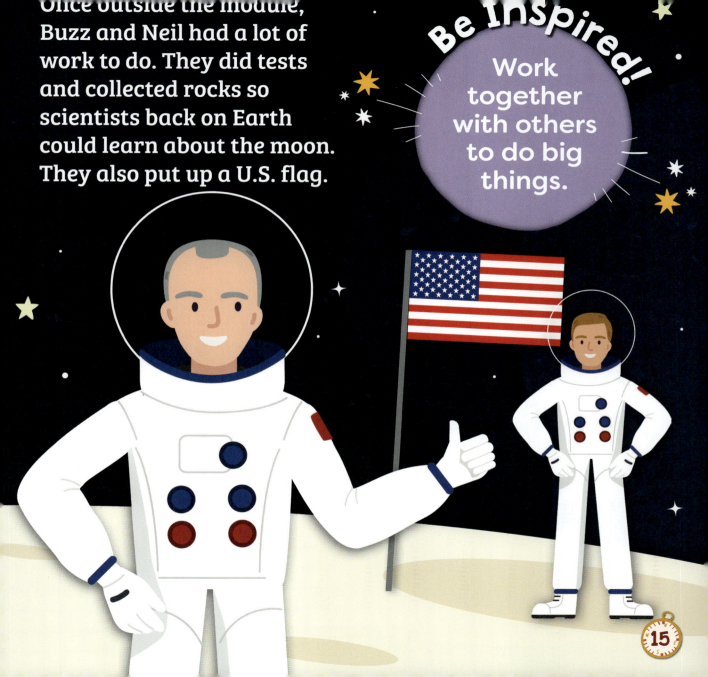

Once outside the module, Buzz and Neil had a lot of work to do. They did tests and collected rocks so scientists back on Earth could learn about the moon. They also put up a U.S. flag.

**Be Inspired!** Work together with others to do big things.

# KATHRYN SULLIVAN

**Born: 1951**

Kathryn Sullivan is no stranger to adventure. She went on three different trips to space. In 1984, Kathryn was the first American woman to do a spacewalk.

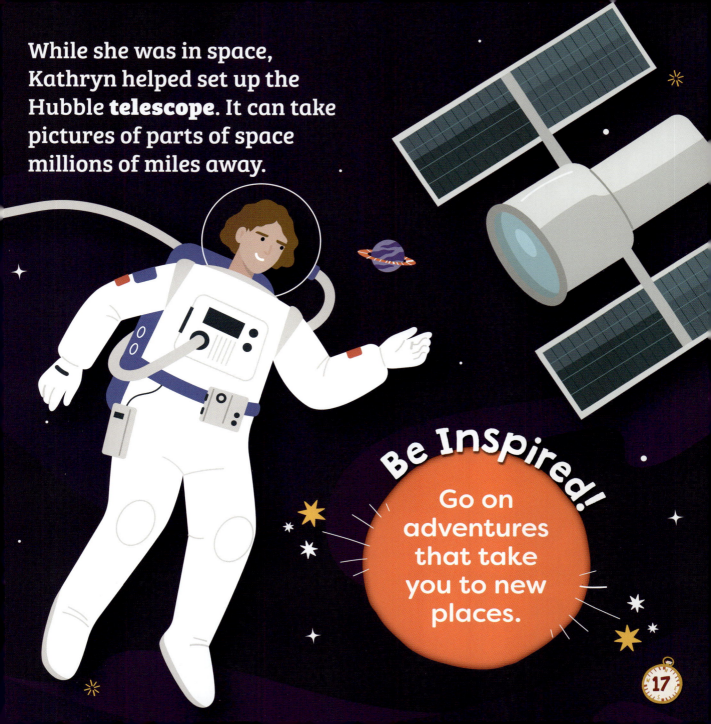

While she was in space, Kathryn helped set up the Hubble **telescope**. It can take pictures of parts of space millions of miles away.

**Be Inspired!**
Go on adventures that take you to new places.

# VALERY VLADIMIROVICH POLYAKOV

**Born: 1942**
**Died: 2022**

Valery Vladimirovich Polyakov was a Russian cosmonaut who spent a lot of time in space. Once, Valery stayed in a spacecraft for more than 437 days!

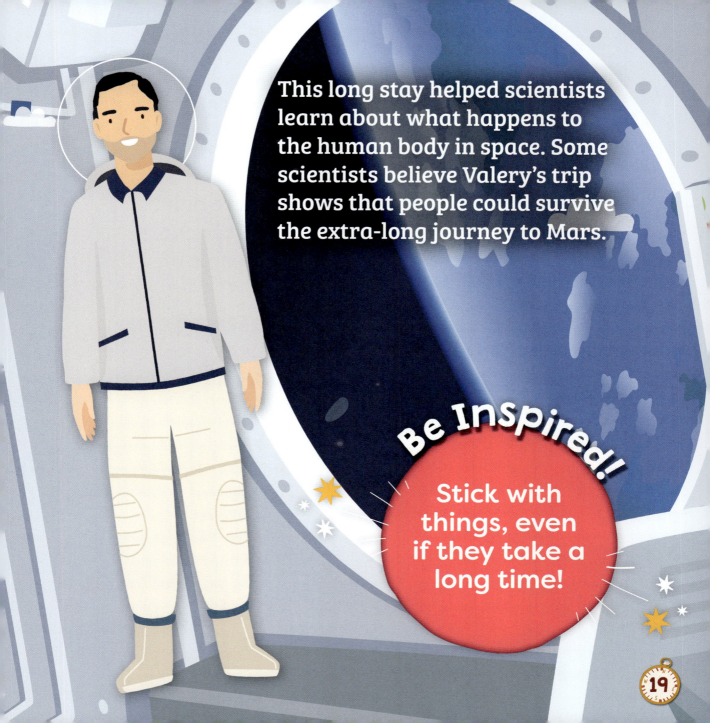

This long stay helped scientists learn about what happens to the human body in space. Some scientists believe Valery's trip shows that people could survive the extra-long journey to Mars.

## Be Inspired!

Stick with things, even if they take a long time!

# YOU

At first, only a few people were able to explore space. Over time, it became easier to safely send more people on trips beyond Earth.

It takes a big team of people to plan a space trip.

Now, even people who are not trained astronauts can go to space. In the future, it may be possible for anyone to go on a space adventure— even you!

# YOUR SPACE ADVENTURE

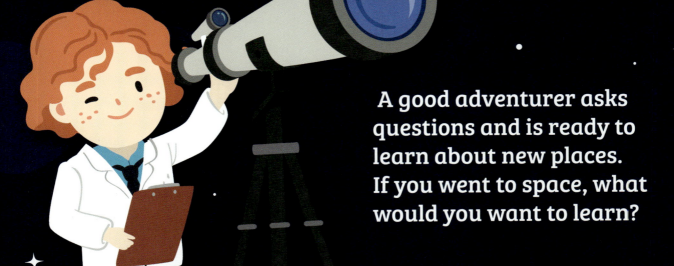

A good adventurer asks questions and is ready to learn about new places. If you went to space, what would you want to learn?

Build your own spacecraft out of paper and a cardboard tube!

1. Roll a piece of paper to make a pointy top.

2. Glue it to a cardboard tube.

3. Decorate your spacecraft and fly it around!

# GLOSSARY

**astronauts** people trained to travel in space

**cosmonaut** a Russian or Soviet astronaut

**lunar module** a smaller spacecraft that travels from a larger one to the surface of the moon

**mission** a plan for a job to be done

**parachute** a soft cloth attached to ropes that is used to slow down the fall of someone or something

**piloted** flew or otherwise controlled a craft

**spacecraft** a vehicle that can travel in space

**spacewalk** a job working outside a spacecraft while in space

**telescope** an instrument that uses lenses and mirrors to make distant objects appear larger

# INDEX

**air** 11
**astronaut** 5, 12, 21
**cosmonaut** 6, 8, 18
**Earth** 6–8, 13, 15–16
**lunar module** 13–15
**moon** 12, 14–15
**parachutes** 7–8
**spacecraft** 7, 9–11, 13, 18, 23
**spacewalk** 10–11, 16
**steps** 13–14
**suit** 10–11
**telescope** 17